BRUCE CARROLL

Sometimes
Miracles
Hide

Stirring Letters from Those Who
Discovered God's Blessings
in a Special Child

HOWARD
PUBLISHING CO.

Our purpose at Howard Publishing is to:

- *Increase faith* in the hearts of growing Christians
- *Inspire holiness* in the lives of believers
- *Instill hope* in the hearts of struggling people everywhere

Because He's coming again!

Sometimes Miracles Hide © 1999 by Bruce Carroll
All rights reserved. Printed in the United States of America
Published by Howard Publishing Co., Inc., 3117 North 7th Street, West Monroe, Louisiana 71291-2227

00 01 02 03 04 05 06 07 08   10 9 8 7 6 5 4 3

Library of Congress Cataloging-in-Publication Data
Sometimes miracles hide : stirring letters from those who discovered God's blessings in a special child /
    [compiled by] Bruce Carroll.
        p.   cm.
      ISBN 1-58229-071-7 (hardcover)
        1. Parents of handicapped children—Religious life.   2. Parents of handicapped children—Correspondence.
    3. Christian life.
    I. Carroll, Bruce.
    BV4596.P35S65   1999
    242'.4—dc21   99-31846
                                                                                   CIP

Edited by Philis Boultinghouse
Cover design by LinDee Loveland
Interior design by Vanessa Bearden

SOMETIMES MIRACLES HIDE/ Bruce Carroll/Word Music (50%)/ASCAP © 1992 Word Music, Inc. and McSpadden Music. All Rights Reserved. Used By Permission.

"Sometimes Miracles Hide" by C. Aaron Wilburn, Bruce Carroll © Copyright 1991. Magnolia Hill Music (50%)/ASCAP/Word Music/ASCAP. All rights reserved. Used by permission of Integrated Copyright Group, Inc.

The letters in this book are adaptations and compilations of letters received by Bruce and Nikki Carroll in response to Bruce's song "Sometimes Miracles Hide." Names, dates, and identifying information in the letters have been changed. The stories were contributed by true-life moms and dads of special-needs children. We thank them for their stories and photos of their children and their undying dedication and love.

The story on pages 76–79 is from *Another Season* by Sally Cook and Gene Stallings. Copyright © 1997 by Gene Stallings and Sally Cook. By permission of Little, Brown and Company, Inc.

Scripture paraphrases in the "Scripture Prayers" are from the HOLY BIBLE, NEW INTERNATIONAL VERSION, © 1973, 1978, 1984 by International Bible Society. Used by permission of Zondervan Bible Publishers. All rights reserved. Other Scriptures are from The Holy Bible, New King James Version (NKJV), © 1982 by Thomas Nelson, Inc.

To all the parents who,
with undying courage and eternal hope,
have kept on keeping on through
sleepless nights,
emotional weariness,
financial strain,
marital stress,
and estrangement from friends

And to all those who,
through the eyes of faith,
have continued to see
God's hidden miracles
and His blessings wrapped in disguise

A very special thank you to
my wife, Nikki,
and my children—
Sarah, Amber, Austin, and Taylor

I want to also thank
Aaron Wilburn for partnering with me in
the creation of the song
John Howard, Philis Boultinghouse,
Denny Boultinghouse,
and everyone at Howard Publishing
Tina Wilson and Special Olympics
Melissa Hambrick, SpinCycle Public Relations
And all the mothers and fathers who chose
to go the distance for their little miracles

"Sometimes Miracles Hide" is a true story about some friends of mine and their journey through a very difficult time in their lives.

Their courage and compassion was the inspiration behind the song; in fact, this song is their story.

I'm humbled and privileged to be a part of a song that has meant so much to so many.

Thank You, Lord, for allowing me to be involved.

Bruce

Dear Bruce,

When my husband and I first heard your song "Sometimes Miracles Hide," we both broke down and cried because you verbalized our relationship with God during a difficult time. We'd like to share with you the story of our "miracle baby," Samantha.

We could hardly contain our excitement as we sat in the doctor's waiting room. "Dr. and Mrs. Lester, we're ready for you now." Our faces beamed as we bounced down the hall to meet the radiologist. The door opened, and there it stood in all its technological splendor. This enormous piece of equipment was introduced to us by Dr. Silers as "The latest medical science has to offer in ultrasound."

Wow! We were impressed! Only the best for Dr. and Mrs. Lester...or so I thought. Then Dr. Silers added: "This technology is now recommended for all moms over thirty-five. The high resolution affords an excellent opportunity to unveil anomalies that otherwise would go undetected."

In one ear and out the other—as I had learned to

do with so many medical mini-tutorials. Doesn't affect us, I thought. Let's get on with it!

The usual gobs of gel and cold breezes passed over my tummy as Dr. Silers and, now, Dr. Lester stood at the ultrasound monitor. Look at this…nuchal thickening…perhaps we had better look for heart defects…yes…endocardial cusion defect…

By now Mark's face was ashen and his expression was visibly burdened, as both doctors looked at each other with overwhelming apprehension. "What's going on?" I asked. "What's wrong? Tell me…what's nu–nu–nuke…the thick…?"

I watched a tear find its way down Mark's cheek as he tried to explain that nuchal thickening alone could mean a 70 percent chance of Down syndrome, but now they had also found "endocardial cusion defects," which meant a 90 percent chance of Down syndrome.

"Our little baby has Down syndrome and a very serious heart defect, Gloria."

"We'll arrange for abortion counseling," Dr. Silers said matter-of-factly. Oblivious to our sorrow and disgust with her statement, Dr. Silers instructed us to follow her down the corridor. In shock we obediently scurried behind her flapping white coat. Suddenly she came to an abrupt stop in front of a door labeled "Psychological Consult Area A." Her icy blue eyes pierced ours as she blurted, "Whenever we have a situation like yours, the hospital's policy is to advise you of your options." Mark and I tried to tell her we were pro-life and that there were no "options"! She totally ignored our pleas as she swung open the door and commanded us to sit on the couch and "get comfortable."

"I don't think you realize the seriousness of this situation. I am going to get the head of radiology; he can give you a second opinion on these findings."

Mark and I positioned ourselves in the center of the purple paisley couch and stared blankly at the Kleenex boxes that lined the coffee table in front of us. Looking into the tears welling up in each other's eyes, we quietly asked Jesus for the right words to penetrate Dr. Silers's heart.

The door opened and the two doctors took their respective brown leather armchairs facing us. They leaned forward in unison. Dr. Silers's brow furrowed as she unsuccessfully searched our eyes for common ground. "We don't think you grasp the gravity of this situation. This is Down syndrome, and you have no idea what it is like to have a disabled child; therefore, you cannot make an educated decision."

The second doctor nodded in agreement.

"Can you tell if my baby is a girl?" I asked.

Dr. Silers looked at me in disbelief. "What does it matter what sex it is? There are much more pressing matters to be dealt with! We don't have a lot of time; you are three and a half months pregnant already. You must look at abortion alternatives to make an informed decision." Her stark blue eyes froze on my face as her impatience was matched only by her determination.

"No thanks!" we reiterated as we jumped to our feet and bolted through the door. Pausing for a moment, Mark turned in their direction and said, "We are Christians and are against abortion, period. We cannot 'decide' to kill our baby! We will pray for God's healing and accept our child regardless of the outcome. We will also pray for strength for others who are presented with your 'alternative' to exchange death for imperfection."

"But…but…we need to do more tests…amniocentesis…and you have to see the geneticist!"

Mark and I briskly walked down the hall, now with both physicians behind us. Mark turned around and retorted, "Current statistics show that amniocentesis may harm the baby. Why would we do that to our child?"

We cried all the way home that wet, foggy September afternoon. Yes, we asked God all the usual questions and experienced the normal denial: Why us? This can't be true! Maybe there was a mistake. And, yes, we prayed, and we prayed, and our church prayed and prayed…always asking God to somehow "fix" our baby. But as we eventually learned, it was us who needed the "repair job," not our child. We are so used to quick solutions and perfection that it took the birth of a beautiful little girl for us to see what God was trying to tell us all along…

"Mommy! Mommy! Look I got a bear! Look, Mommy, look!" Samantha's big, green eyes search mine for approval, and then she runs off in a half-skip down the hall.

Sometimes miracles do hide; just ask anyone who has had the privilege of running head-on into Samantha's abounding good cheer. To say she is "special" is not just a cliché to make us feel better. When God gives a family a special-needs child, He gives them the most important gift of all: love, unconditional love.

Five souls were transformed the day Samantha came into our lives. Through her, God showed us that we were prideful and distracted by our worldly accomplishments. Through the veil of God's mercy, we watched our hearts melt in a pool of compassion for our little girl. We came to understand what Jesus meant when He said, "Let the little children come to me, and do not hinder them, for the kingdom of heaven belongs to such as these."

For our family, every day is a blessing, a new adventure, and sometimes an opportunity to share Samantha's story with others. We thank the Lord for entrusting us with His precious gift—love. The compassion God gave us for Samantha has spread to the homeless, those in prison, others with medical needs, and individuals whom this world labels as "less desirable." And our newfound compassion is just one of a million reasons why Samantha is a blessing. Having a child with Down syndrome is not something we should pray to "go away"; rather it is a privilege that God entrusts us with. It changes our lives and, in turn, the lives of others.

God has opened many doors of opportunity for Mark and me to speak publicly, not only about Down syndrome, but also about our pro-life stance. As Christians we know the two issues are closely entwined. For three years, now, we have played your CD

"Sometimes Miracles Hide" for our audiences. A dry eye is a rare find during your Spirit-filled, heartfelt, compassionate song.

Mark and I want to say thank you for listening to your heart when God called you to write this song. Most of all, we thank Jesus for giving you the talent to reach so many hearts.

In two months Samantha will be five years old. She is beyond a doubt the apple of Daddy's eye (and knows it!). A lot has happened in five years, but one of the most life-changing, significant events was the first time Mark and I held each other's hand and listened to you sing out loud the song that God had put in our hearts.

Sincerely yours in Christ,

Dr. Mark and Gloria Lester

Jason, Jess, Brad, & Samantha

They were so excited
It was coming to be
Two people so in love
Now soon there would be three

Dear Bruce,

When my son, Marshall, was born, in many ways I felt as if he were my little "Samuel," for I had hoped and prayed for him for years. But my precious little son was born at the end of my fifth month of pregnancy. He was the smallest thing I'd ever laid eyes on. He weighed one pound, thirteen ounces and was as long as a ruler. The doctors gave him only a 25 percent chance of survival.

At the time I found it very hard to believe that God had intended this nightmare for my good. But through this trial, the Lord has taught me about letting God be God and accepting His will for my life.

I'll never forget the evening when the doctor informed my husband and me that Marshall had bleeding in his brain and as a result would have brain damage. I'd never felt so alone and abandoned by God. I was scared and angry and felt totally defeated.

But on our way home from the hospital, the most beautiful song I'd ever heard came over the radio. My tears freely flowed as I listened to the words, and I felt as if God were speaking directly to me through your song. It seemed that God was saying, "Yes, Marshall is going to be handicapped, but he is also going to bring you great joy—a joy greater than you have never known." I felt a peace in my heart and soul that I hadn't felt since the day I asked the Lord to be my Savior. Your song helped me accept God's will for me and my son.

I guess I will "have to wait a lifetime to see the reasons with my eyes," but frankly, that isn't so important to me anymore. I am just enjoying the son I was blessed with and am thankful for God's refinement in my life. And I am thankful to the Lord for using you and your talents to ease my pain and the pain of many other parents of handicapped children. You will never know the blessing you have brought our family.

Even now, two years later, when I am having a particularly hard day in caring for Marshall, I just pop in "Sometimes Miracles Hide" (affectionately called "Marshall's Song" in our house), hold my son close, and sing my heart out. It always makes me feel better and reaffirms God's love for me and my son.

Your sister in the Lord,
Alice Heath

All Things

And we know that all things work together for good to those who love God, to those who are the called according to His purpose.—Romans 8:28

"What do you mean all things? How could this be for my good?" I have to admit I have asked myself that question on more than a couple of occasions. When my wife was diagnosed with cancer, I asked. When we lost almost all of our worldly possessions in a fluke fire, I asked. When I was burdened with debt because of a business manager who wrecked my finances, I asked. Through these things and many more, I've been faced with the ultimate dilemma: *Do I trust God?* And the answer comes back a resounding *yes!* Let me tell you why I do. I trust Him because I have history with Him. He has proven to me over and over again that He is faithful.

Sometimes there are no easy answers, but His promise remains true. He may not take our trials *away*, but He'll always take us *through*. He's always here, always will be. Our faith is made real when we share in His suffering. I'm sure He knew what we would face. In fact, the Word says He has already faced all that we have faced and ever will. He has overcome the world.

So when you find yourself asking *why?* cling to Romans 8:28—it's for all of us. We will get past the pain, and when we do, we'll see that God was there all the time.

Bruce

Jesus,

    I am feeling burdened, and so I come to You for rest and refreshment of my soul. I willingly take Your yoke upon myself, and I open myself up to learning of You. I know that You are gentle and humble in heart, and I am confident that You will bring rest and relief and quietness to my soul.

    I believe that Your yoke is pleasant and that Your burden is light and easy to bear. I commit my life to You, O Eternal God, and I cast all my burdens on You, believing with all my heart that You will sustain me and will never allow me to fall.

    Enable me to be still and rest in You. Slow me down so that I can wait patiently on You and lean on You for all my strength.

—Matthew 11:28–30; Psalms 55:22; 37:7

Your Weary Warrior

For many years they'd planned it
Now it would soon be true
So she was picking out the
   pink clothes
And he was looking at the blue

Dear Bruce,

When I first heard your song "Sometimes Miracles Hide," I thought, How did he know what happened in my life? Is he reading my mind?

Our life starts out just like your song. We were so excited when I found out I was pregnant. I wanted a girl and John wanted a boy. I was four months pregnant when I had an ultrasound. We learned, then, that our baby had a terminal birth defect called anencephaly. They suggested that we terminate the pregnancy. Instead, we prayed that God would heal our baby.

Joseph David was born on a beautiful fall morning, and the doctor's fears were immediately confirmed. However, he was a miracle baby because he lived for two days. The doctors could not believe that he lived that long.

I still haven't discovered all the blessing God has in store for us and why He allowed us to go through this, but I do know that He will work all things together for our good, and I pray that someday He will use our experiences to bless others.

Every time I hear your song, I think of my "little blessing," who is in a far better place than I am. I look forward to the day when I can see him again.

Keep us in your prayers. We keep you in ours.

Sincerely,

Marge Young

Scripture Prayer

Dear Father,

I come before Your throne with confidence and boldness, believing that I will receive mercy from Your hand and find the grace I need to get through this time. I claim Your promise that Your grace is sufficient for me; I believe You when You say that Your power is made perfect in my weakness. Therefore, Father, I boast in my weakness so that Your power may rest on me. I proclaim and believe that You are able to make all grace abound to me so that in all things at all times, You will supply me with all I need. I give it all to You, Father, and trust it to Your care.

—Hebrews 4:16; 2 Corinthians 12:9; 9:8

Confidently Yours

Grace comes into the soul,

as the morning sun into the world;

first a dawning; then a light;

and at last the sun in his full

and excellent brightness.

—*Thomas Adams*

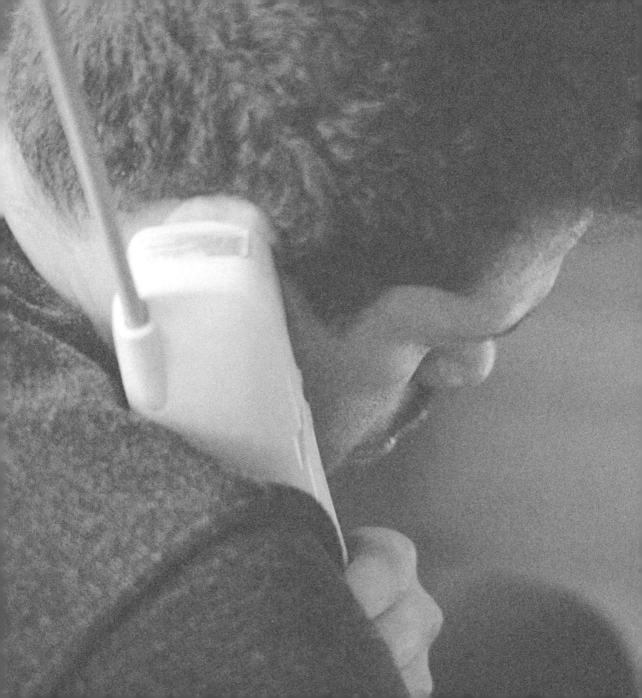

The call came unexpected
The doctor had bad news
Some tests came back
    and things weren't right
He said, "You're gonna have
    to choose"

Dear Bruce,

The first time my wife and I heard "Sometimes Miracles Hide," we cried. To this day, I cannot hear the song without tears flowing.

Liz and I have an autistic son, Bobby, who has multiple handicaps and is extreme and violent at times. Because no one knew about his condition before he was born, we were not pressured to have an abortion. But since Bobby's birth, many people—including doctors, schoolteachers, administrators, even members of our own family—have pressured us to "put him away."

"It would be so much better for the family," they say. And to convince us, they remind us of the high divorce rate in marriages with handicapped children.

As Bobby grew, his behavior became even more extreme, and we were very much pressed. Yet God was greater than our darkest circumstances. We believed that God creates no accidents and that Bobby was His gift to us—even though we didn't know how it all worked.

Despite the internal and external pressure to quit,

we knew that God had not given us a throwaway child. We held firmly to our belief that God wanted us to care for and love Bobby with all our might.

And as the years have passed, we have begun to see God's hidden miracles in the blessing of Bobby. His smile can brighten up a room, and now that his behavior has calmed down dramatically, he brings so much joy into our lives. To play off what our Lord said of Nathanael, Bobby is a child "in whom there is no guile." Bobby has no hidden agenda, and the longer I am in ministry, the more I come to appreciate people whose cards are all on the table.

The Lord has used Bobby to make us grow up in ways I don't believe Liz and I ever would have, if given the option. And the Lord has used this song to remind us of the truth of His sovereignty and grace and mercy—truths we really needed to know.

We have since passed your song on to other couples who are dealing with similar issues. We know it has blessed them in the same way it has blessed us.

May God bless both you and your wife for your faithfulness to Him. We thank you for being a blessing to us.

Your brother and sister through the love of Y'shua,
Harry & Liz McDaniel

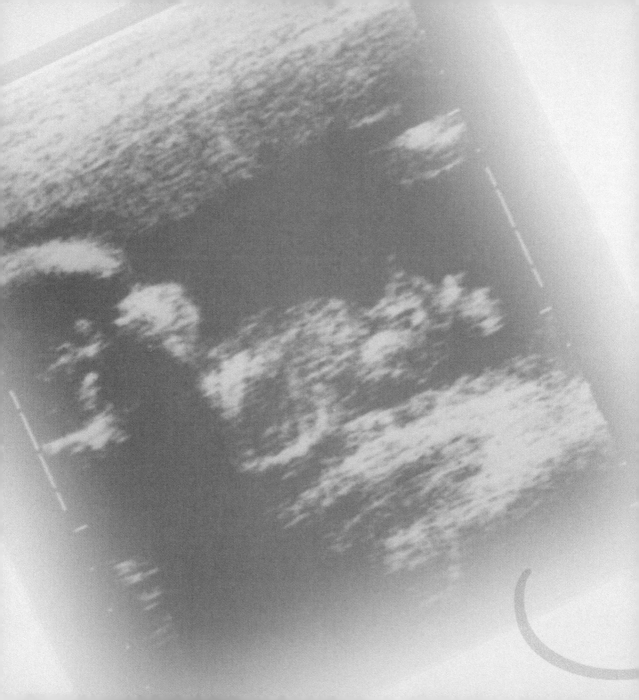

"I'll wait a week for your decision"
Then the words cut like a knife
"I'm sure everyone will understand
If you want to end its life"

Dear Bruce,

I was four and a half months pregnant with our third child when my husband and I found out through a routine ultrasound that our precious little baby had anencephaly. We were both totally shocked, as we already had two perfectly healthy children at home. The technician performing the procedure told us that our best option was to terminate the pregnancy. We were fortunate to have an obstetrician who supported us in our decision to take the baby to term. He sent us to a specialist to confirm the baby's condition.

The specialist, however, was not so supportive. He told us we were crazy to continue with the pregnancy. When we told him that we loved our baby and were going to keep him as long as we possibly could, he said this was not an ethical matter. The way he put it was that our baby "was not compatible with life." He insisted that it would be in our best interest to terminate the pregnancy immediately. He couldn't begin to comprehend why we would make this choice. But even then, like your song said, we believed we could hear God's voice encouraging us with the thought that "sometimes miracles hide."

Next, we were sent to a genetic counselor and a genetic doctor. The counselor was great. She explained what anencephaly is and how the baby's brain would never develop. She told us what our baby would look like. She supported our decision to continue the pregnancy, but she emphasized that it would be very hard on me emotionally to carry a baby for five more months, knowing that he would die at birth. I appreciated her honesty and candor, but with each discussion our conviction intensified.

When the genetic doctor came through the door, the first thing my husband did was to tell her that we were keeping the baby and that we didn't want to hear anything about an abortion. The doctor turned to me and said, "We're talking about your body and your choice, not your husband's. What do you want to do?" She said the baby was going to die anyway and that it would be easier on everybody to just get it over with now. Why should I put myself through all that pain and emotional suffering when the outcome was so grim? She told me that the baby might die during the birth process, and if not, it would most likely die ten to twenty minutes after birth.

The next five months were very hard. The baby grew and began to be very active. How could such a strong, active baby have such a devastating birth defect? My husband and I knew we couldn't possibly get through this difficult time without our church, family, and friends. We knew God was on our side, that He would help us through this, and that He would never leave us.

We prayed for a miracle. What a great miracle that would be! Wouldn't it be great if we could show all those doctors and doubting people that Jesus healed our baby? We also prayed for strength, then we turned it over to God for His will to be done. We prayed that we would be able to use this experience and our baby's life in His plan.

When I went into labor, thirty people were in the waiting room praying for us. As I lay there waiting for the baby to be born, I knew we had received our miracle—we were having a baby, and birth is one of the greatest miracles of all. I also knew in my heart that my baby would die.

At the moment of our precious little Matthew's birth, I felt an intense peace and joy. Matthew survived the birth process and was breathing on his own. We were blessed to spend eleven wonderful hours with our little boy. He stayed with me in my room the entire time, knowing only the comfort and love of his mother's and father's arms. Right before he died, he seemed to be seeing angels coming to take him home. He died very peacefully.

My husband and I know in our hearts that we made the right decision to carry our little blessing to term. The time we had with him was so special. He drew us closer to the Lord and made our relationship with each other even better. We know that one day we will be with our child again in heaven. What a glorious day that will be, to see Jesus and our Matthew!

Because of my experience, I have been able to let the Lord use me to help two other women who also chose to take their anencephalic babies to term. They said it was so helpful to talk to someone who knew what they were going through.

A friend gave me a copy of your song "Sometimes Miracles Hide" two weeks before my son was born. I can't express to you enough how much that song meant and continues to mean to my husband and me. It was as if you had us in mind when you wrote it. The song reminds us that we are all special miracles.

May God's blessings be upon you,

Terry Lerue

Unfailing Mercy

Oh give thanks to the Lord, for He is good! For His mercy endures forever.
To Him who led his people through the wilderness,
for His mercy endures forever.—Psalm 136:1, 16

Our difficulties are always matched by God's mercy. We are never left alone to fend for ourselves.

We all have "wilderness" experiences at some points in our lives, but we are never alone. We are always surrounded by the immeasurable, merciful hand of God.

Sometimes God gives us a gentle push of courage; sometimes He mercifully numbs us so we don't experience the full intensity of our pain; at other times He carries us when we cannot take another step on our own.

From the many letters I've received from the parents of special-needs children, I've learned that God provides His people with superhuman strength to survive excruciating pain and suffocating disappointment.

Even in the desert, God's mercy is there. The trials of this life will not last forever. Frail, imperfect bodies will be made perfect and whole. Tears and defeats will dissipate. Mourning will be turned to joy.

May we be found faithful until the end. May we ever rely on His abundant mercy. May we allow His faithfulness to beam through us and lighten the burdens of others.

Bruce

Gracious Father,

Some days I am amazed at the wisdom I see reflected in my "simple" child's face, and then I remember that You reveal wonderful and marvelous things to little children—things that are hidden from the "wise and learned." No wonder my child has that knowing look. Help me to become more like my child in the qualities that are precious to You, for I know that the kingdom of heaven belongs to little children just like mine. Help me to always remember how precious my child is in Your sight—so precious that You know exactly how many hairs are on my little one's head. Even though it's sometimes difficult, I praise You for the honor of serving "one of the least of these," for I know that when I love my child, I am loving You.

—Luke 10:21; Matthew 18:3; 19:14; 10:30; 25:45

Lovingly Yours

Though they were badly shaken
They just had no choice
They knew God creates no accidents
And they were sure they heard
　　His voice saying

Dear Bruce,

 The first time I heard you sing "Sometimes Miracles Hide," I was in my kitchen with my husband and two daughters, and I broke down and cried. I felt as if the song had been written just for us. You see, our four-year-old daughter, Maryann, was born with multiple disabilities due to a very rare genetic condition. She is beautiful and loving, but as yet she cannot crawl or walk or speak. Her muscle tone is very low, and she has little functional use of her right hand. It is hard to know how much she understands, but it is more than she can express.

 Early in my pregnancy, ultrasounds showed the possibilities of problems, so we lived with uncertainty for several months. Only my husband's consistent affirmation that "any child God gives us will be a gift" brought me through that time. When Maryann was born and we were told her diagnosis, God quickly assured me that she was special just as she was and that she was not a mistake or accident. So your words "God creates no accidents" had a very special meaning for me.

Over the last couple of months, I have been struggling (as I do periodically) with fear for Maryann's future and especially with uncertainty for my own life as a mother and a Christian. For eighteen years I have been a physical therapist, working with children who have special needs. Now my own child's needs coupled with those I work with threaten to overwhelm me. Because of our financial needs, quitting my part-time work is not an option.

Your song reminded me (and continues to remind me) that although we may not understand why God allows pain to enter our lives, we can know that He works all things together for our good. It also reminds me that somewhere out there other Christian couples are facing what we face, struggling as we struggle. This thought is precious to me since I have no Christian friends in a similar situation who can share and understand my experience.

Thank you for writing the song and allowing God to use you in this way. And please thank your friends for sharing their story in the words of the song. I covet their prayers.

In Christ,
Sharon Marshall

Dear Father,

Evening, morning, and noon I cry out in distress, and I know that You hear my voice. For You have promised that You will deliver the needy who cry out, the afflicted who have no one to help. And I believe with all my heart that You will work all details of my life—the good and the bad, the joy and the sorrow—that You will weave all these together for my good. Since You are for me, no one can successfully stand against me; because You did not spare Your own Son but gave him up for me, I know that You will graciously give me all that I need. I have full confidence that nothing can ever separate me from Your love—not trouble or hardship, not sleepless nights or lack of progress. I know—because You have said it is so—that I am victorious in You; I am even more than a conqueror!

—Psalms 55:17; 72:12; Romans 8:28, 31–32, 38–39, 37

Victoriously Yours

*T*he steps of faith fall on the
seeming void and find
the rock beneath.

—*Walt Whitman*

Inspiration

Sometimes miracles hide
God will wrap some blessings
in disguise

Dear Bruce,

I am writing this letter to express my grateful appreciation and to affirm how God has used your music in a truly beautiful and somewhat mysterious way. I assume the purpose of your song is to comfort parents with less-than-perfect babies or even to encourage them to choose life rather than abortion.

However, it spoke to me in an entirely different way. The first time I heard it, I was driving in my car and tears began streaming down my face as God spoke to me through the words "Sometimes miracles hide."

I'm the youngest of six children, the unplanned "accident." My nearest sibling reminded me many times over the years that I wasn't "wanted"—and I don't recall either of my parents ever denying that assertion. I'm forty-two now, and I've carried shame and the feeling of being unwanted for many years. The feeling of being unloved was buried so deep in me that it has taken lots of time and therapy to bring it out and deal with it.

As I listened to your song that first time, I became

the hidden miracle. It no longer mattered that I was not wanted or that I was an "accident." God made me, I am His miracle, and He wants me more than I could ever imagine.

Your song literally changed my outlook on life. I've become a rather busy person—I volunteer at our church's Mothers' Day Out program, and I go to college full-time (my love for learning has been reborn). I am a happier wife and a better mom to my two teenage sons. I thank God daily for their understanding as "Mom" has had to spend quite a bit of time getting herself together—and I thank God for Christian music, which is so very powerful.

We just never know how God will use us to help others in their journey.

Thanks so much for what you do,
Lila Telford

Mom!

Aliscia Banks

When Liles was first diagnosed with spinal meningitis, I saw no hidden miracles. The first three months of his life, I was overwhelmed with fear and sorrow and thought only of survival—his and ours.

Before Liles was born, Steve and I were in complete control of our lives—or so we thought. Our careers were in order, our future was planned, our finances secure. Everything was going our way, and we had no reason to think things would not continue just as we'd planned.

Liles was born January 7, 1987, a healthy five-pound, fourteen-ounce, bouncing, baby boy. When he was born in 1987, hospitals were just beginning the policy of pampering new moms. I had a beautiful room with a TV and was served a delicious steak dinner after Liles's birth. It was wonderful!

We took Liles home when he was five days old and loved our son like any new parents love their child. But when Liles was just ten days old, our whole world changed. After nursing Liles, I laid him down for his nap. Two hours later, when I went to check on him, I was horrified at his appearance. He was a ghostly shade of gray. He had diarrhea, and he was moaning—a terrifying sound.

I snatched him up and ran to the living room. "There's something wrong!" I cried to Steve, who was sitting on the sofa. His first reaction was to think that I was being an overprotective, overanxious new mom, but I knew something was terribly wrong.

Our pediatrician met us at the emergency room. Liles had only a slight fever, but before the doctor did any tests, he guessed that he had spinal meningitis. By now his brain was beginning to swell and was visibly protruding from his fontanel. The spinal tap confirmed the doctor's diagnosis.

Liles was immediately put into ICU. He was already almost comatose, but they gave him a drug to completely immobilize him. He needed all his energy for healing. He had eight different lines in his little body.

During those first three months, we lost him twice. Twice they had to do "cut downs"—a procedure used when the need for a specific drug is so urgent that there's no time to wait for an IV; they just slashed him to insert the tube directly into his artery. Once on his arm and once on his leg.

Our days were filled with one trauma after another. We would go from one burst of bad news to the next.

I'll never forget an encounter with a neurologist that truly undid me. It's never good news when you're dealing with a neurologist anyway. That alone was enough to shake me severely. But up until this point I had managed to keep it together.

I remember being led into a small conference room. There was one table in the center and one window on the outside wall. The neurologist matter-of-factly held up an x-ray of Liles's brain, directing his gaze at us as if we could interpret its contents. I didn't have a clue what it showed. Impatient with our ignorance and our lack of understanding as to the severity of the problem, he explained that every place we saw black on that x-ray was an empty cavity where Liles's brain used to be. Even I could see that most of his brain was destroyed.

But something in me prevented my comprehending the severity of Liles's condition. The whole experience had taken us totally by surprise, and I had been unable to absorb the implications. Something in me kept thinking, *If I could just get Liles out these hospital doors and into our home, he'll be all right.* And for some reason, the only thing I could think to ask this belligerent doctor was, "When will he open his eyes and look at me?"

With cold, unfeeling eyes, the neurologist stared into mine: "You don't understand, Mrs. Banks. It won't matter if he ever opens his eyes. Even if he does, he will never know you are his mother."

That's when I lost it. It was the most horrible thing a person could say to a mother. And when he went on to advise that we "put him in a bed and have another baby," I went over the edge; I was hysterical. With unfeeling control, he stuffed a piece of paper in my husband's pocket with his name and phone number on it and said, "Call my office when you get her under control."

But God is so good. The neurologist had tried to strip my motherhood from me, but God set out to confirm my value and His love. At the very moment the neurologist was ripping my heart out, my pediatrician was in the hospital making rounds. When some nurses saw the state I was in, they immediately paged her, and she came straight to me. She wrapped her arms around me and rocked me like a baby while I cried. Moments later my minister joined us. He, too, just "happened" to be in the hospital. Then, some kind nurses asked me if there was something—anything—they could do to make me feel better. I immediately knew what I needed. We hadn't been able to hold Liles because of all the tubes in him. Now, with the prognosis of impending death, it was no longer important that Liles remain in his safe, sterile Isolette.

They picked him up, wrapped his tubes all around him, and placed him in my arms. For the first time in months, this mother got to hold her son. The minister, using a small Styrofoam cup, christened our sweet little boy. I rocked him and held him and was instantly and completely filled with happiness and peace. For the first time since the ordeal began, I felt the Lord's healing in my soul.

But guess what. Liles lived! And guess what else! He calls me "Mom" nine thousand times a day. He wraps his arms around me and squeezes me so tight that sometimes it almost hurts. When he gets off the school bus at the end of his day, he is as proud to see me as if I'd been gone a year. He squeals at the top of his lungs, "Mom!"

I used to play a game with God where I would ask Him to take either Liles's physical or mental disability away. And in my game, I would have to choose which one God would take. I always ended up in the same place. I would always have God take away his physical disabilities. For his mental disabilities have shaped his sweet disposition. He is the most loving, happy, congenial, genuine child I know—and he will probably be this way his whole life.

He wakes up singing every morning. And when I come into the room, he says, "Start me off, Mom!" and so I count for him, "One...two...three..." and he begins. I never know what he's going to sing. It could be "Happy Birthday," "Jesus Loves Me," or "Amazing Grace."

I would never wish the heartache and disappointment associated with a child like Liles on anyone, but I can honestly say, without reservation, that he is a blessed gift of God and I am so thankful he is ours.

I often think of a scene when Liles was about a year old. We used to sit him in the corner of our overstuffed couch. His balance wasn't very good, and the corner of the couch propped him up just fine. It was one of his favorite places to be. Steve would often sit in the room with him, either on the couch beside him or on the floor in front of him, leaning on the couch. One day when the three of us were in there together, Steve said, "You know, when it's just us, he seems so normal." Those words spoke volumes to me.

So much of Liles's "disabilities" are merely in the eyes of the beholder. The fear and ignorance of others label him "abnormal," but when we're away from those labeling eyes, he is perfectly normal.

Who's to say whether a special-needs child is more difficult to raise than a "normal" one? Twelve short months after Liles was born, our second child, Molly, entered the world. To this day I often wonder how I ever conceived her. Steve and I were hardly ever alone. Our lives were consumed with Liles. But here she came. And she's been a blessing ever since. But just as Liles presents special problems in rearing, so does Molly. Neither one of them is really more difficult than the other—they're just different.

Life doesn't always turn out like we expect or want it to. When Liles got sick, this was the first serious obstacle that either Steve or I had ever encountered. We went from being in "total control" to being "totally out of control." We had no place to go but down—down on our knees before God. We could do nothing but hit the floor, and that's what we did. There were times when I screamed out my pain to God. We were so powerless, we were forced to go to Him. He was our only hope.

But to this day, I've never asked *why?* My mother always taught me not to say "Why me?" but "Why not me?" God does not purpose our little ones' lives to be less than their full potential, but when a life is damaged or made sick by the natural conditions of this fallen world, God redeems all the pain, if we will but bring it to Him. He faithfully brings miracles of joy and love out of hiding and into the light.

You may have to wait this lifetime
To see the reasons with your eyes
'Cause sometimes miracles hide

Dear Bruce,

The first time I heard your song "Sometimes Miracles Hide," I fell in love with it and immediately drove to my Christian bookstore and bought your CD. Every time I listen to it, it makes me cry. It was as if you wrote it just for me.

Seven years ago, we had our fourth child. Ryan has Down syndrome, and he has truly been a "miracle" child. He came close to dying three times before he was one; he survived open heart surgery and complications from that surgery, three other surgeries, RSV, and pneumonia. In all, he was in the hospital eight times before he was twenty-one months old.

My husband, three children, and I are all Christians and are very involved in our church. Like you said in the song, we don't know why God allowed us to have Ryan, but I am so very glad that He did! It was hard for our friends and family. My brother still hasn't talked to me since Ryan's birth. He just doesn't know how to handle Ryan or our "special-needs" family.

Several friends sent us cards saying that we must be special because God gave us one of his special children. At the time, we didn't feel very special. Now we do. Not only has Ryan changed our lives, but he changes everyone he comes in contact with. He makes everyone smile.

Watching Ryan interact with other people is one of my favorite "blessings in disguise." Uninhibited and overflowing with unconditional love, Ryan runs up and hugs anyone and everyone—without reserve, without prejudice. Other children, adults, the elderly—Ryan loves everyone. Maybe we all could learn more from these children.

I have shared your song with other parents of Down syndrome children. I wanted to thank you and let you know how much your song is appreciated.

Thank you,

Marci Hawkins

Eyes Straight Ahead

Brethren, count it all joy when you fall into various trials, knowing that the testing of your faith produces patience.—James 1:2–3

I have to admit to being very cynical at times. Sometimes I think I'm the only one whose boat has a hole in it or that my problems are more overwhelming than everyone else's. But when I start playing the "poor me" role, the Lord always has a way of bringing me back to reality.

Not long ago, the Lord convicted me to seek to find joy in my trials. So I began to search. It didn't take me too long to figure out that one of the reasons I couldn't find joy was because I was looking in the wrong place. I was looking at myself and my trials. I was not looking at Jesus.

Proverbs 4:25 says, "Let your eyes look straight ahead, and your eyelids look right before you." Verse 27 says, "Do not turn to the right or the left; remove your foot from evil." The Lord began to reveal to me that if I would look straight ahead, my eyes would be fixed on Jesus. But because I was looking to the left or right, I was actually walking down the path of evil. Rather than focusing on Him, I was focusing on my circumstances or on what people said or did. I knew that if I didn't overcome this hurdle and gain victory, I'd never find the joy I was searching for.

God reminded me that Peter was empowered to walk on water as long as he kept his eyes on Jesus. But as soon as he took his eyes off the

Lord and focused on his circumstances, he began to sink. As long as I stay focused on the Lord Jesus, I am not only in His will, but I experience His joy. As I walk in His victory, my outlook on life becomes useful in the lives of others, who, like me, are also enduring "various trials."

Now, when my eyes begin to wander, Philippians 4:8–9 comes to mind, and I willfully transform it to my heart by obedience: "Finally, brethren, whatever things are true, whatever things are noble, whatever things are just, whatever things are pure, whatever things are lovely, whatever things are of good report, if there is any virtue and if there is anything praiseworthy—meditate on these things. The things which you learned and received and heard and saw in me, these do, and the God of peace will be with you."

When I realize how much God must trust me to allow me to experience such great trials, I'm amazed. And when I willfully count my trials "all joy," He gives me the gift of patience to help me through the next round. He thinks of everything!

Bruce

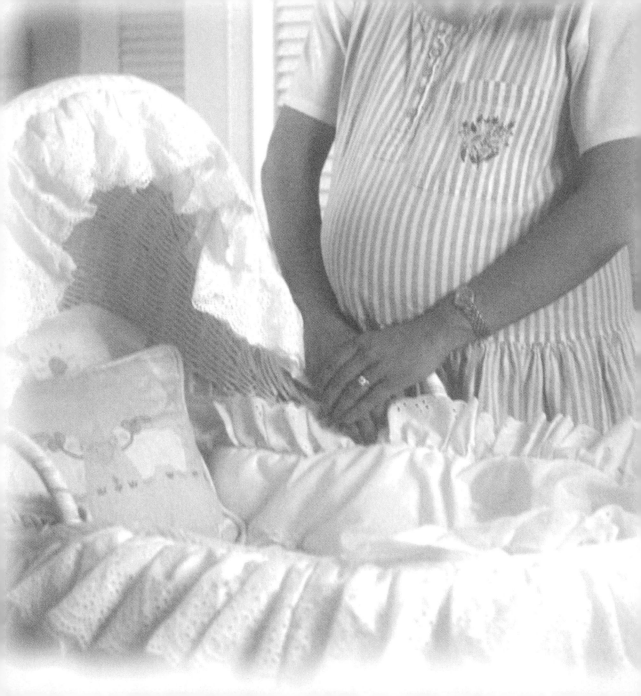

It seemed before they knew it
The appointed day arrived
With eager apprehension
They could barely hold inside

Dear Bruce

The first time we heard "Sometimes Miracles Hide" was in a funeral service for our friends' precious baby, who had a chromosome abnormality and lived only four months. Little did we know how much your song would soon come to mean to us as well.

We were so excited to find out we were pregnant with our second child. The pregnancy seemed routine and normal until an early sonogram revealed that my baby had a severe abnormality and would not live for more than one week after birth. My whole world crashed around me.

Of course there were those who "advised" us (although we did not ask for advice) to terminate the pregnancy. But abortion was not an option for us, for we believe that God creates and loves all human life.

So for the next seven months of our pregnancy, we loved our baby while we could and tried to prepare for her expected death. As you can imagine, this was an extremely difficult time, but God's presence was very real.

On February 16, Anne Marie Allison was born and died during delivery. We were "hard pressed from every side, but not crushed."

We know that God is sovereign and faithfully fulfills His promises. Without Christ and His redeeming work on the cross, we would have no hope. But we do have hope, and we know that Anne Marie is with our Lord in heaven and that we will see her again someday.

Of course, we had "Sometimes Miracles Hide" played at Anne Marie's memorial service. I doubt that there was a dry eye in the church, even though several of our non-Christian friends were there too.

Although we don't yet understand or see God's purposes clearly, we have peace in our hearts about releasing her to live with God, and we have confidence that we will see her again.

Many in our society have no patience for "hidden miracles"; they prefer to see miracles flash right in front of them. But it is often through unanswered prayers and hidden miracles that we learn the most about God. Thank you for putting this story so beautifully to music. Please keep up the good work and keep strong in the Lord.

Because of Him,
Margaret & Tom Allison

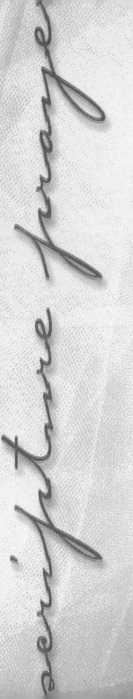

Dear Father,

I am feeble and utterly crushed; I groan in anguish of heart. I am completely spent. But I know, Lord, that You are close to the broken-hearted and that You save those who are crushed in spirit. And so I know that You are close to me now. I have been hard pressed on every side, but not crushed; I have been perplexed, but not in despair; I have been struck down, but not destroyed. I believe that because I trust in You, I will never be put to shame. I will be strong and brave, for my hope is in You, O Lord.

—Psalms 38:8; 34:18; 2 Corinthians 4:8–9; Psalms 25:3; 31:24

Undefeated

$\mathscr{P}$ain when properly handled
can shape a life
for greatness.

—Charles Swindoll

The first time they laid eyes on her
Confirmed the doctor's fears
But they held on to God's promises
'Cause they were sure they both could hear

Dear Bruce,

Our son, Hunter, weighed only three pounds, thirteen ounces when he was born. He was born early, and we knew he would be small, but neither we nor our doctor had any idea he would be that small. The first time we laid eyes on him, we were terrified, to say the least. He was barely breathing, his color was unnatural, and he had multiple tubes running through his body. According to his doctor, he had distinct signs of a genetic disorder. We were devastated.

But we knew—no matter what—that God had a plan for Hunter's life (no matter how short it may be) and for ours. Hunter's first days were an uphill climb, but he survived the odds our doctors had given us. His genetic testing—placed on a forty-eight hour rush—took over a week.

Three days after our son had surgery, we learned that he had a deletion on his number two chromosome. The doctors had no idea what it meant but could only tell us to expect the worst and hope for the best. They were certain, given the rarity of his disorder and the fact that it involved the second-largest chromosome, that he would suffer physical and developmental disabilities, likely in the "severe" category.

There were times when we didn't feel we could face another day, but God always wrapped His big arms around us and carried us through. He gave us faith, and He gave us our family, friends, and a loving, ever-prayerful church family. Their prayers, love, and support carried us when we could not walk alone.

After a month in the hospital, and a few trips back and forth, Hunter was finally home—we prayed—to stay. It was during that summer that a friend from church saw your song printed in a magazine, cut it out, and sent it to me.

After reading it, I just knew God was telling me that despite Hunter's prognosis, everything was going to be all right. The next day, I went out and bought your tape. I've listened to it at least once every day since.

"Sometimes Miracles Hide" is a song about love, faith, joy, and dreams. It's about the dreams all parents have for their children—which may or may not be in God's plan. It's about having faith in God's plan when yours are turned inside out. It's about love—the love for God's wisdom and for a child. And it's about joy—the joy you receive when you look into the face of the child God gave you and know that your love for that child is unconditional, just as our Father's is for us.

Hunter is now a cute little one-year-old. He is behind in his development, but he is much further along than the doctors had anticipated, and he works really hard at physical therapy once a week and every day with Mom!

God gives us all kinds of blessings. Sometimes they are right in front of us, and sometimes they are wrapped in a disguise. The quality of a person's life cannot be measured by how much they have accomplished, but by how much love they can give. Hunter already has a high-quality life.

I pray God will continue to enable you to minister to all those out there who are searching for the love and peace of our Lord and Father.

God bless you!
Shiela Pauls

$\mathcal{F}$aith goes up the stairs that love has
made and looks out of the window
which hope has opened.

—*Charles Haddon Spurgeon*

inspiration

Sometimes miracles hide
And God will wrap some blessings
in disguise

Dear Bruce,

I first heard your song as I was driving home from a doctor's visit. The doctor had confirmed I was indeed expecting our sixth child! Being thirty-seven years old, I was quite surprised. Somehow we'd thought our "quiver" was full with five!

I cried at the words of your song, for they spoke of every mother's "fear"; yet they also spoke of the hope that comes from knowing that God is in control—even in difficult times.

Nine months later, we discovered the "miracle" that the Lord had been hiding inside my womb. Tests confirmed that our little girl had Trisomy 21, Down syndrome. I cried more tears, holding our little miracle in my arms—so uncertain of what tomorrow would bring.

But the words of your song returned to me again, reminding me that God's hand was indeed in our lives. Your song reminded me to trust Him…because sometimes miracles truly do hide and surely this was a blessing in disguise.

Sherry Grace is now three years old and is a constant source of joy to our whole family. Every day we see more evidence of the hidden miracles tucked in her generous, loving heart.

I just wanted to thank you for making a difference in our lives with such a beautiful song!

Sincerely,

Maxine Peters

Strike One

Gene Stallings

—from *Another Season: A Coach's Story of Raising an Exceptional Son*

In the late fall of 1975, we received a letter from Johnny's school declaring that his class was going to be mainstreamed in physical education in a few months. The children would be playing softball. I had no idea what mainstreaming was or how it worked and I felt some anxiety as I read and reread the letter.

Whenever I heard that Johnny was going to try something for the first time, my initial reaction would be one of pure happiness and excitement. But then after a while I'd start getting nervous, and inevitably I'd end up worrying over whether he'd be accepted, or if he could physically handle the challenge, or if people would tease him. It bothered me that I was so overly protective, and I knew, of course, that if I was going to do the right thing by Johnny I'd have to let go a little more.

A couple of months later, we received a note from Johnny's teacher that softball would be starting soon and that Johnny had been chosen to be the pitcher of his team. All of the fears that I had about him playing softball suddenly vanished and I felt proud and excited. I went out and bought new bats, gloves, and bases the next day after work, and now when I'd get home the children and I would practice softball in the backyard and Johnny would always be the pitcher....

I was surprised to find that Johnny had a lot of natural ability.... He had a good strong arm, took his time, and was consistent, and I found myself bragging about his new position on the team to anybody who would listen. He loved the game, there was no doubt about it, but what he talked about most were his friends.

One warm spring afternoon I decided to leave work an hour early and go watch them play. I drove out to his school, making sure that I parked my car in the lot farthest away from the playing field so that Johnny and his teachers wouldn't see me. Then I walked out to the side of the field and stood next to a big maple tree.

Johnny stood a few feet off the pitching mound, outfitted in a bright blue vest, and I could see that he was really concentrating as he slowly wound up and then pitched a perfect ball to a cute little redheaded girl who also had Down syndrome.

"Strike one!" the teacher yelled. The outfielders, dressed in the same vests as Johnny, shouted, "Strike her out, Johnny! You can do it! Strike her out!" Johnny paused, looked back at his team members, and smiled.

Johnny wound up and pitched again. The redheaded little girl belted the ball. I watched the ball fly up in the air, right above Johnny's head. Then I held my breath and watched as he paused, looked up into the sky, and then almost as an afterthought stuck out his mitt at just the right angle and caught the ball. There was loud cheering from the outfielders as they ran in and patted Johnny on the back.

When it was his turn up at bat, he swung hard at the first two balls that were pitched to him. But when the next pitch came at him, he connected, whacking it good and hard. He stopped, watched as the ball bumped along the field past the shortstop, and then he gently placed the bat down on the ground. I watched as he shuffled off to first base and I thought how the doctor said he no longer needed to take digitalis, his heart medicine. We never tried to stop him now from doing anything physical. But as the outfielder scrambled to throw the ball to first I noticed that Johnny's face was very pale. His skin was the color of pearls and I could see as he landed on base how breathless he was.

"Safe!" called the teacher-umpire as Johnny stood solidly on the base. The next batter was an able-bodied little girl who hit a long fly ball way past the right fielder. Johnny got mixed up and started running toward third base, but one of the children dashed out to the field and led him to second, third, then home as the batter followed patiently behind Johnny. His team won 3–0, and his teammates jumped up and down, picked each other up, yelled, and carried on.

That night at the dinner table he talked about the game and how his team had won and then he went on and on about all of his friends. As I sat there and listened to his happy chatter that night, I doubt you could have found a prouder father in Dallas.

You may have to wait this lifetime
To see the reasons with your eyes
'Cause sometimes miracles hide

Dear Bruce,

Eleven years ago, in late February, I conceived a daughter. At the time I was a backslidden Christian and was not married to her father. He was recently divorced and very bitter. I believed that I could change him and make everything all right.

When I found out I was pregnant, I was very happy. I thought that by having his baby, I would prove to him that I loved him. But his reaction was not what I expected. He wanted me to abort our baby. I was devastated!

Even though I had left many of my Christian convictions behind, I managed to hold on to my belief that abortion was wrong. I just knew that the child I was carrying was the little girl I had always dreamed of having. Her father threatened to commit suicide when I refused to have the abortion, but I told him that he was an adult and that if he chose to kill himself, it wasn't my fault. The baby growing inside me couldn't choose, and I wouldn't choose to end its life.

When I told him I was considering adoption for our baby, he said, "But what if the baby is retarded or something? No one will want it then."

I assured him that if no one else wanted my little baby that I would keep it and that I could give it all the love it would need. But he was bent on my having an abortion, and he started making threats. I feared for my life. A neighbor helped me get away from him while he was at work. My brother sent me a bus ticket, and I moved to Arizona to have my baby.

I did investigate putting the baby up for adoption, but by the time I was five months pregnant, I had decided to keep it. And my baby was a beautiful little girl. At the time, she seemed so perfect. But as time passed, it became more and more evident that she wasn't. My beautiful little girl was retarded! Her father had spoken it, and it had come to pass.

There were times, while still in my backslidden state, when she was the only thing that kept me alive. When I'd think about ending my life, I would think of her. I was all she had. I had heard on the news about other women killing their children and then themselves, but I couldn't take her life—no matter how desperate I felt. So I decided to focus on her and live for her.

When Heather was five years old, I found the Lord again, and everything began to change for me. I began to live again, only this time in Christ. I may have lost the Lord, but He obviously never lost me. God's hidden miracle was already at work.

When Heather was six, I met and fell in love with a wonderful man of God. We were married when she was seven. He loves her as if she were his own. To look at the two of them, one would never know she wasn't.

Heather has been diagnosed as moderately retarded. They don't know the cause and probably never will. She has vocal apraxia, though she loves to try to sing. She has ADHD and behavioral problems. It is hard on us at times.

Every time I get down about her, I eventually stop and think how special she is. Your song reminds me of that, and I'm able to keep going and not give up. Thank you!

Someday I hope to be able to sing this song for someone else who needs to hear it. That is, if I can ever get through it without crying.

Your sister in Christ,
Jenny

P.S. Maybe God will use Heather to save her father.

*M*aturity begins to grow when
you can sense your concern
for others outweighing your
concern for yourself.

John McNaughton

Trusting Faith

Trust in the LORD with all your heart, and lean not on your own understanding.
—Proverbs 3:5

Scripture tells us that, in this life, our view of reality is like a blurry reflection in a mirror, but that someday, we will see God clearly, as He really is—and we will see Him face to face (see 1 Corinthians 13:12).

Our earthly eyesight is just too imperfect to see down the road far enough for this life to make sense. That's when trust takes over. God does not expect us to understand all of life's circumstances. In fact, He tells us *not* to rely on our understanding, but to trust in Him.

So when you're tempted to ask *why?* or when your heart wants desperately to make sense of it all, remember Proverbs 3:5. You don't need to understand. What you need to do is trust in the Lord.

When trust turns into praise and when we open our mouths to thank Him for His goodness, something supernatural takes place inside our worried souls—we find peace and strength. We forget about ourselves and instead focus on the One who holds the whole world in His hands.

When we stop striving to "understand" and give in to trust, we will see that His mighty hand was at work all along in the thing we thought would crush us. Not only will we perceive a new reality, but we will rejoice in it.

Bruce

Creator God,

I know, Lord, that the child You have given me is fearfully and wonderfully made. I praise You for this blessed gift, for I know full well that Your works are wonderful. You reached into my womb and knit this child with Your own hands. I know that as long as I hope in You, I will never be put to shame.

But sometimes, Lord, I feel afraid, and I need to feel Your presence. I need to feel Your hand in mine, leading me beside still waters, where I can be refreshed and made new. I seek a peaceful bed in green pastures where my soul can be restored. On my worst days, I feel as though I'm walking through the valley of death, yet even then, I will fear no evil, for You are with me. No matter what today brings, I know that Your goodness and love will follow me. And I know that I and my sweet child will dwell in Your house forever.

—Psalms 139:14, 13; 25:3; 23:2, 4, 6

Trustingly Yours

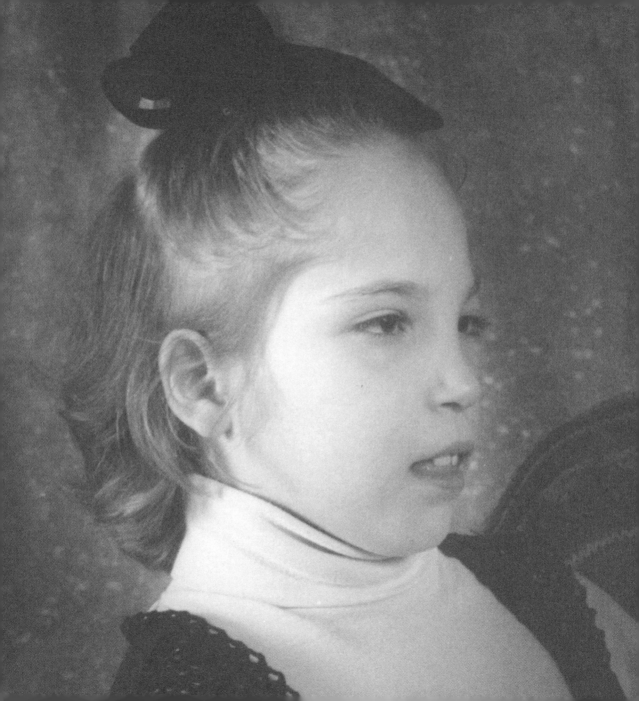

Though she was not
like the other girls
They thought she
was the best
And through all the
years of struggle
Neither whispered
one regret

Dear Bruce,

Your song "Sometimes Miracles Hide" has touched our entire family. When our cousin's baby was born with water on the brain, the doctors predicted that she would not live and if she did live, that she would be completely non-functional or, as one doctor put it, "a vegetable." When Marci was born, we began to discover the extent of her problems. We called everyone we knew and asked them to pray for her welfare—people all across America were praying for her.

Today, Marci is our family's "miracle baby." Those first few months after she was born, our whole family cried together, waited together, and prayed together. As we did, we grew closer to one another and closer to God. Because of Marci, our faith in God has multiplied; we really believe that if God had not stepped in, Marci's condition would be much more severe.

Like the couple in your song, we laugh and cry when Marci does something the doctors said she wouldn't be able to do—such as walk, talk, and attend school for special children! We praise God every time she proves them wrong.

Your song completely captures our family's feelings for our special gift from God! Marci is almost four years old now, and we think she is the best and cutest kid around! We would not give up the gift of Marci for anything in the world. It is our prayer that your song can help others see the "miracle" of these special children.

Thank you again for the beautiful song about God's "miracle babies." May God bless you and your ministry for the work you do bringing His glory out in song.

Yours in Christ Jesus,

Jim & Sarah Lewis

Hey, That's All Right

Mike Cope

It was one of those days when I was resenting Megan's "condition." I had taken her and her older brother to a baseball card show. At the time, there was nothing her brother Matt would rather do than look at, trade, or (if it was my money) buy baseball cards.

But when I tried pushing Megan in her oversized stroller through the narrow aisles, she kept grabbing legs. Then she started reaching for the cardboard gems with names like Nolan Ryan and Ken Griffey Jr.

So out we went to the playground. That's where we met Jason. Six years old. A child for whom "Twenty Questions" is a way of life.

"Hey, what's your name?" he asked Megan.

"Her name is Megan."

"Hey, can you swing next to me?"

"Well, she can't handle that kind of swing very well. Let's try this one with a safety bar."

"Hey, you want to go in the tunnel with me?"

"Let me get her out of the swing and we'll see."

"Hey, how come you keep answering for her?"

"Megan doesn't talk much."

"She looks old enough to talk. Why doesn't she?"

"Have you ever heard of being retarded?"

"No. But why doesn't she talk?"

"Well, Megan is almost seven, but in the way she thinks—and talks—she is more like someone who's two."

"Hey, that's all right. Megan, let's go through the tunnel."

Sometimes big theologians can come in compact sizes! Jason had pretty much figured it out. Our version of the all-American kid is inadequate: the rookie league all-star, the whiz kid who reads at age three, the precocious survivor who thrives even if left "home alone."

Even our language betrays our misguided values. We speak of "gifted and talented students." Megan obviously wasn't one...unless, we mean someone "gifted and talented" in areas like compassion, forgiveness, and kindness. Then she could have been a valedictorian.

Not every child is an early reader, a spelling-bee winner, or a Mark McGuire on the Little League field.

"Hey, that's all right." Jesus loves all the little children of the world!

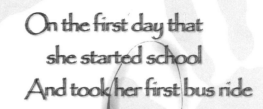

On the first day that
she started school
And took her first bus ride

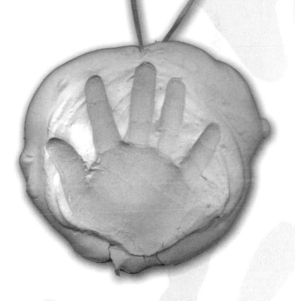

They remembered the words
that God had spoke
And they both broke down
and cried

Dear Bruce,

My life is in your song. When I first became pregnant, I had no idea what the Lord had in store for me and my beautiful baby girl. I had never given any thought to the possibility of having a handicapped child. I had never even been around someone who was handicapped. I thought handicapped children were born only to people who took drugs or something. Surely that could never happen to completely normal me!

After an emergency C-section, I delivered a precious baby girl. We named her Liana Rose. The doctors and nurses calmed all our fears about the C-section and told us that Liana was perfectly normal. She was certainly the most beautiful baby I had ever seen.

At nine months we began to notice that Liana was not sitting up or trying to crawl. As naive new parents, we thought it was because her grandma and grandpa (who kept her while I worked) held her all the time.

Just before she turned one, we took her to the pediatrician to see if anything was wrong. We were stunned when the doctor told us that he thought she had a brain tumor! His supposition was shortly proven wrong, but that was the beginning of an emotional roller-coaster ride.

When Liana was just thirteen months old, she was accurately diagnosed with cerebral palsy. But she was so perfect looking! How could this happen? Didn't God love me? Didn't he love my baby girl?

Looking back, it's a wonder that my marriage and my sanity survived all the extreme ups and downs. We were told, and willingly believed, that her case was very mild and that with just a bit of therapy she would walk and talk. So what if she couldn't win the Olympics? During this time I was also dealing with the grief of three miscarriages, and we were having frequent money worries. But surely, with just a little more therapy, Liana would walk, just a little more time and she would talk…

No.

No.

Her progress was very slow and painfully gained. We soon had to accept that she would never walk or run or dance, and her speech was all but impossible to understand. Our goals were lowered again and again. Now, we simply hoped to get her out of diapers.

When Liana was five, I had a healthy baby boy. About this time, my husband, Allen, became a Christian, and we prayed and prayed for Liana. We took her to healing services and had others pray for her and us. Doesn't God love innocent little girls? Was I being punished for something? How could God be so cruel? There were times when I was very mad at God for not healing Liana.

After yet another miscarriage, it seemed that we would not have any more children. Boy, can I laugh at that now! God was just beginning something unimaginably wonderful in our lives, and He would use Liana to do it!

My heart broke every time the neighbor kids came to ask if Liana's little brother, Lyle, could come out and play, while Liana was ignored. Then I noticed a lively little girl in a wheelchair who rode the bus that Liana took every day to her school and therapy. The bus driver mentioned that the little girl needed a place to stay while her father was out of the country. I thought she might be the perfect friend for Liana. That was how Kelly came into our lives. Through a series of circumstances, we had Kelly for almost four years. And so began our career as foster parents.

Over the next ten years, twenty children came through our home. We had babies, teenagers, hurt ones, handicapped ones—every kind of challenge you can think of and some you can't. God was using us in a miraculous way; we saw healings of every kind.

We noticed that Liana loved each and every one of these children with her whole heart. She accepted them just as they were—unconditionally, unreservedly. She taught them and us that there was no one we couldn't love, no matter how unlovable they seemed. She taught me that everyone has something to give and that God can use anyone. Liana, who has almost no ability to care for herself, showed me how to care for others. My innocent little lamb loves with the love of Jesus.

My, how God has used her! I know now that God is not cruel. He is infinite in love and goodness. Of all the things that I would not have chosen, having a handicapped child ranks at the top. Of all the blessings in my life, Liana has been the greatest, and she has taught me that "the greatest of these is love."

The most important thing I've learned from Liana is that we're all handicapped and that God loves us just as we are. He does not need to heal us and make us perfect in order to love us. If we were all perfect, we would not need Him and we would not need each other.

By the way, it has occurred to me that when the abortion of handicapped babies is discussed, the parents of handicapped children are never asked for input.

Allen & Alicia Roberts

He'll Be All Right

Iris L. Sheets

He was born prematurely on a Tuesday morning in 1953. I saw the doctor cut the cord, and I heard a faint cry. He was so tiny, and he had heart and respiratory problems, so he was placed in an incubator for fifteen days.

All alone in the hospital because my husband was working out of town, I cried day and night for my sick little baby. On Good Friday, early in the morning, a bearded man came into my hospital room. He looked at me and softly said, "Don't worry about him. He'll be all right." And then he was gone. I never saw him again.

We named our son Martin David, and we call him Marty. With lots of tender, loving care, he survived his first dangerous weeks, and we thought all was well. But when Marty was three and a half, he was diagnosed with Down syndrome. We were heartbroken. How could this happen? Why hadn't he been diagnosed sooner? The doctors told us he would never be able to tie his shoes or button his shirt. But I immediately set out to prove them wrong. I taught him to do both that very afternoon!

When his IQ was tested, his was the highest of any Down syndrome child they knew of at the time. His father and I decided then that we would teach him to always do the best he could.

Marty graduated from high school in 1972. That same year, he started work in the stockroom of what is now Hecht's department store. Just recently, he was awarded with his diamond star pin for twenty-seven years of service.

Marty's life has not always been easy, but it has been filled with victory. He is faithful to his Sunday school and church. He often serves as usher or greeter and sometimes gives the prayer of thanksgiving during the morning worship. Marty is very athletic. He swims, water skis, snow skis, bowls, lifts weights, and plays golf. In 1968, he was chosen to attend the first international Special Olympics held at Soldier Field in Chicago. Since then, he has traveled all over the country, participating in Special Olympics sports events.

In 1995, I got an unexpected phone call two days before Marty and his father were scheduled to leave for the World Games in New Haven, Connecticut.

A Special Olympics associate was calling to ask if I was planning to come to the Games. When I told him I wasn't coming since Marty wasn't competing, he asked if I would change my mind if I knew I would be sitting with President and Mrs. Clinton! We had been chosen to represent Special Olympics families by sitting with the Clintons during the Opening Ceremonies. Talk about surprised! My first thought was, *What am I going to wear?*

When the day arrived, we all took our designated seats in the president's box with thirty others. Among the dignitaries were members of the Kennedy family, U.S. senators, several diplomats from others countries, Sargent and Eunice Shriver (she is the founder of Special Olympics), and the great soccer player, Pele.

Marty's designated seat was directly behind the president and beside Pele. His dad and I were one row back and over to the side. As the ceremonies were about to begin, I noticed that Marty was having a serious discussion with a man in a blue suit. I could tell by Marty's expression that he was troubled. Soon the man in the blue suit came over and asked for my help. He explained that he was a Secret Service agent and that it was his responsibility to sit directly behind the president. But Marty's nametag was on that seat, and Marty didn't want to move. It had his name on it, and that was that! It took some talking, but we finally convinced Marty to scoot over a bit, and everyone was happy.

The sick child I cried over in my hospital room so many years ago is now one of the greatest blessings our family has known. How thankful we are that that once tiny, pitiful baby, who was not supposed to tie his shoes or button his shirt, has found victory after victory in his God-blessed life.

I frequently think back to the message from the bearded "stranger" in my hospital room who said, "Don't worry about him. He'll be all right."

See to them it just did not matter
Why some things in life take place
They just knew the joy they felt
When they looked into her face

Dear Bruce,

From the first time I thought about having a little girl, I knew what I wanted to name her: Angela Joy. But it was not to be—at least not for a long time. For ten years, my husband and I tried to have a child, but month after month, year after year, we faced disappointment.

The yearning to have a child can be a powerful emotion—especially for a woman—and I struggled with depression off and on through the years. Only by the Lord's grace did my heart and marriage survive the discouragement I felt.

When I found out that I was finally pregnant, I was overcome with joy. My husband and I and my whole family were so excited. Then came the devastating news: Our little Angela Joy had Down syndrome. All my dreams of the perfect little girl vanished. How could I give her the name I had chosen so long ago? I felt anything but joyous. Depression threatened to consume me. The day I learned the news was the saddest day of my life.

But then one Sunday morning, I heard your song

on the radio. One line changed my whole outlook: "They just knew the joy they felt when they looked into her face."

God changed my heart right there and then. Angela Joy is now seven years old, and she is truly the joy of our lives. She is a precious gift from God.

Thank you for the song that opened my heart to the joy God had in store for me all along.

Sincerely,
Barbara Deville

Victorious Heart

Christine Burke

Our little miracle is named Nicole Victoria Burke. We gave her that name because it means "Victorious Heart." And a victorious heart is exactly what she needed.

She was born in Korea as an orphan with severe heart problems. Medically, her condition was called tetralogy of Fallot, meaning four major malfunctions of the heart. She was also born without a right hand.

She not only needed a heart repair and quickly, but she also needed a family. We were the lucky ones who got the call. At the time of the call, my husband, Tim, was playing for the Montreal Expos, and we just happened to be in Chicago—where he was playing against the Cubs. How perfect; she would be arriving at the Chicago airport.

When she came off that plane, our eyes flooded with tears. Our little girl was finally here. She was so serene, so beautiful, and we loved her so much already.

We immediately flew back to Montreal, which was home at the time. Unfortunately, we had to wait longer for Nicole's surgery than we had anticipated because of scheduling conflicts, but finally the day came for her life-changing surgery.

Because Tim was traded to the New York Mets the day before the surgery, he could not stay. Without a doubt, it was one of the hardest days of my life. I held Nicole close. I prayed, I cried, and then I released her into the arms of the pre-op nurses. I was so afraid. When I kissed her good-bye, I knew it might be my last kiss.

Eight hours later, the surgery was over, and it was a complete success! I rushed into ICU to see her and was shocked by the color of her toes and lips; they were pink instead of the purple I'd become accustomed to! She looked great! I wanted to hold her, but the thirty-something tubes and wires she was hooked up to prevented that. So I just sat next to her and rubbed her hair and kissed her angelic face. I couldn't wait for her to wake up.

The day finally came when I got to hold her. She was awake and had most of the tubes out. But something about Nicole was different. She didn't cry; she just stared. When I put a bottle to her lips, she wouldn't suck. When I put a spoon of food to her mouth, there was no response. "What has happened to my little girl!" I demanded to know. The doctors finally ran some tests on her brain, only to get horrible results. Sometime during or after surgery, Nicole had suffered severe brain damage and would be profoundly retarded for the rest of her life.

What a nightmare. What a tragedy. To make matters worse, Nicole began to have brain seizures. Some thirty, forty, fifty a day. Her body would stiffen up, then she'd come crashing to the floor. Sometimes she would crash her head into my chest so hard that I was afraid she would break her nose. Her crib sheets were often covered with blood in the mornings from her crashes. We got a helmet to protect her head, but it couldn't protect her face.

Through the following months, we tried every medicine known to man to help control the seizures, but to no avail. We tried steroid shots in her upper thighs; we tried special diets. The only thing left was brain surgery, but we just couldn't bring ourselves to put her through that yet.

We felt hopeless and depressed and didn't know what to do. Thankfully, somebody else did. And those somebodies were much younger than Tim and I and evidently a lot wiser too. They were our two children, Ryan and Stephanie, and they were only five years old.

That year we had begun to teach Ryan and Stephanie to pray. We'd gotten them special prayer journals and had taught them to draw a picture of the person they were praying for. Over and over Ryan and Stephanie drew Nicole's head in their prayer journals, and they told us they were praying that Jesus would heal her brain.

Being wise "spiritual parents," we told them they should start praying for other things. We didn't want them to be disappointed with God when He didn't heal Nicole.

Thank goodness, they disobeyed. Because, one morning, Nicole woke up to a brand-new life. Dramatically and miraculously, her seizures had stopped.

Within a few months, our little three-year-old took her first steps. There was no more blood, no more blackouts, no more falling.

The next few months were filled with dramatic steps of growth for Nicole. She began to coo and gibber for the first time since her surgery. As the years passed, she learned to hold a spoon and feed herself; she learned to walk, run, roll balls, clap her hands, and drink from a cup. She has even learned to say something we thought we'd never hear, "Momma and Dahhdee."

We used to wonder if Nicole would ever be able to go to school and learn. We wonder no longer. Last week our little seven-year-old did the impossible—by her doctors' standards, that is. They said our little girl might never hold a pencil, utter a spoken word, or be able to learn—but Nicole proved them all wrong. With her pencil in her hand, she scratched lines onto a piece of paper while she muttered the letters N..I..C..O..L..E. And at night, if you listen carefully, you can hear Nicole singing "Silent Night" as she lies in bed. She has even learned to mutter, "I…Wuuuvv…Uuuu."

But there is a difficult side to Nicole. She is very psychotic at times, and as she gets older, she's gotten more aggressive and has frequent violent episodes. When Nicole was three and a half, she became more demanding and her episodes of violence and aggression increased. At this time, Tim made a bold decision. He decided to retire from his successful career in major league baseball and stay home to help me raise our children. Though he travels some on speaking tours, he spends most of his time at home with me and our children.

The stress of having a special-needs child brings much strain to a marriage. Statistics say that 70 percent of couples with such a child end their marriages in divorce. Although in most families at least one of the parents must work outside the home, I am thankful that Tim was in a position to stay home with us.

A few months ago, Nicole was having a particularly psychotic time, and we were having to give her medicine every couple of hours. We had to hold her down and restrain her in order to calm her down. It often took both of us working together. During one of those times, I was stroking her hair and rubbing her back, trying to soothe her, and I was overcome with an awareness of the miracle of our Nicole. I looked over at Tim and said, "I'm so glad God chose me to be Nicole's mother. It is such a privilege. You know how Jesus said, 'When you do these things to the least of one of these you do it to Me'? Well, to many people, Nicole is the least of the least. When I'm rubbing her back or stroking her hair, I'm doing it to Jesus. What an honor! What a miracle."

Miracles hide, and then someday when you least expect it, miracles shine. When they do, God gets the glory and we get to enjoy the work of His hands. I praise the Lord for His kindness to our little Nicole and our family. I praise the Lord also for people like Bruce who sing the words that give parents like us something to hope for and hang on to.

They learned sometimes
miracles hide
They said, "God has wrapped
our blessing in disguise"

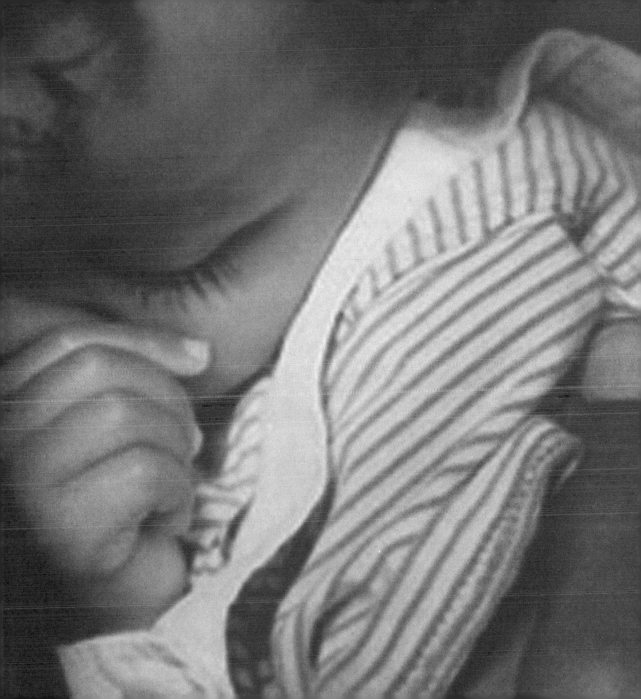

Dear Bruce,

I have been a Christian for seventeen years and am
an associate pastor's wife. My middle child, Brook, has
Down syndrome.

Several years ago, I sought counseling for some serious problems with anger and a past abortion during my teen
years. As my counseling progressed and memory blocks dis-
solved, it was evident that I had been abused sexually as a
child. I became angry at God and blamed Him for allowing
me to be hurt in this way. But I also blamed myself for
aborting my child, and I contemplated suicide as punish-
ment. I could not forgive myself, and I struggled with my
faith in God. I could not comprehend a God who would
allow such abuse.

I brought a friend to your concert in hopes of lifting
her spirits because her brother has AIDS. As the evening
progressed, I was inspired by your faith and trust in God!
The most thrilling moment was when you said that God had
asked you to sing a song that hadn't even been recorded yet
for someone in the audience. And then you sang

"Sometimes Miracles Hide." I wept out loud as the song confirmed that God had His hand on my life! I talked with you for about thirty minutes after your concert, and you said you would pray that God would reveal His grace and His plan for my life.

Here's what He has done since your prayer for me: First, He revealed that He saw me while I was being abused and that it hurt Him just as it hurt Him when Stephen was stoned. Then He revealed to me the role of "free choice." I began to understand that just as I was the one who chose my abortion, my abuser was the one who chose to hurt me—not God. God loves and wants only good for me. In fact, He loves me so much that He allowed His pure, innocent Son to be abused by the very ones He came to save. God is so good!

Once the walls of shame and blame were broken down, God began to speak to me and my husband, and He put a desire in our hearts to open a home for pregnant girls. Sixty-five days later we moved onto the property God had chosen and sold our house for cash in two weeks!

Thank you for being obedient to God's leading. Now you know the results.

In God's grace,
Sherry Marsh

Angel

Joe Beam

No one laughed at her the day she graduated. No taunts. No mockery. Maybe they were too focused on their own achievements to remember to ridicule the retarded girl. Or maybe she just looked so radiant, so beautiful, that even the least sensitive among them couldn't bring themselves to mar her special moment.

Throughout her school years, Angel endured hurtful words from a handful of fellow students whose IQs were higher than hers but whose hearts were much, much smaller. As changes in life brought her to different schools, the names and faces of her tormentors changed, but the insults didn't.

"Daddy, what's a retard?" or "Mom, what's a dummy?" she would sometimes ask, tears streaming down her face as she came in from school. But on her graduation day, all of that was forgotten, relegated to the realm of unpleasant memories that deserve no afterlife.

Technically, Angel didn't graduate from high school. In our state, special-education students may attend school until they are twenty-one, learning

from their dedicated teachers about important matters like the value of money,

reading, and other specific life skills. Then they participate in graduation with that

year's crop of seniors. Instead of diplomas, they receive certificates of completion.

Scanning the line of incoming caps and gowns, I stood ready to click the

record button as soon as Angel came into view. But when I saw her, my hand fal-

tered, and the picture on the tiny screen jostled crazily.

It wasn't just her smile of unadulterated joy that nearly dropped me to my

knees. It was an instantaneous, deeply emotional realization that what we'd taught

Angel her entire lifetime was true. She is different in some ways, but she can dream

and work and achieve just like all the rest of us. God may have gifted other people

differently than He did Angel, but He used just as much care and thoughtfulness

when He chose Angel's special gifts as He does with every other person on this

planet. She isn't mentally handicapped because God forgot her or ran out of mate-

rials the day she was born. Whatever the causes of her mental disability, God gifted

her for His own unique purposes. He made her a marvelous example of a human

who gives unconditional love and gentle acceptance.

With careful words, we'd told her that so many times. In plainer language I'd lectured large audiences with the same truths—not just about my daughter but about all our children, handicapped or not. But it was when she walked across the stage with that Cheshire cat grin that I finally felt the truth I'd spoken a thousand times. Our Angel was proving to us that mental retardation was a limitation of life only if she—or we—let it be. When they called her name, "Angela Michelle Beam," and she crossed that stage to take her certificate, Alice and I wept openly, ignoring the surprised stares and whispers from nearby seats.

Angel believed what we taught her about her abilities even more than we did. Maybe that's why she carries absolutely no recollection of the taunts from her school days. They have no reality for her because she knows they aren't true. She knows that she can do anything her heart sets itself to do.

She has the graduation pictures to prove it.

You are valuable because you exist.
Not because of what you do or
what you have done, but simply
because you are.

—Max Lucado

We may have to wait this lifetime
To see the reasons
   with our eyes
But we know sometimes
   miracles hide.

Dear Bruce,

When our son was born with life-threatening heart problems, we wrestled with the loss of our dreams. We had such high hopes for him, such plans! But it didn't take long before God broke through our disappointment and filled us with love for our precious baby boy.

After ten days in NICU, our tiny son was able to come home with us while we awaited the right time for his heart surgery. After he'd been home a couple of days, some friends, who also had a little baby boy, came over with a special piece of music someone had shared with them. They had never heard it, but thought we would be blessed by it. The song was "Sometimes Miracles Hide."

As we listened, tears of joy and pain streamed down our faces. No matter how many times we listen to it, we feel the tears come and we recognize afresh the precious gift that God has given to us. We quickly determined that we wanted that song played at Joshua's dedication at church.

But that was not to be. Joshua died before the dedication took place; we had the song played at his funeral instead. Our youth pastor sang it and sounded as if he'd been singing it all his life. You would have been proud.

During my son's brief life, your song was a source of great comfort. I have shared the lyrics with a number of others—parents of kids with Down syndrome and Internet friends who prayed often for Joshua before, during, and after surgery.

I know of two children—and there may be more—whose parents made the decision not to abort, in part, due to Joshua's story. I know that our time with Joshua was more joyful because of the message God brought to us through your music. Thank you again. I praise God for your talents and what they have brought to so many.

Jeb Hazelton
Proud papa of Joshua

We've learned sometimes miracles hide

May God bless you as you continue to discover His hidden miracles in your life. If you listen for His voice, look for His help, and long for His appearing, you will sense His presence in every battle, victory, sorrow, and joy.

For personal appearances, workshops, or concert information, please phone the Greg Oliver Agency at 615-790-5540.

For information on other CDs by Bruce, E-mail Bruce at guitaroman@aol.com.

If you'd like to write Bruce and share your own miracle story, write to him at P.O. Box 128040; Nashville, TN 37212.